Original title:
Nimble Sprigs Around the Elf Lash

Author: Olivia Oja
ISBN HARDBACK: 978-1-80562-450-9
ISBN PAPERBACK: 978-1-80563-971-8

Secrets Tucked in the Roots' Embrace

Beneath the earth, whispers stir,
Ancient tales of what once were.
The roots entwine, a bond so deep,
Holding secrets that shadows keep.

In the stillness, a soft sigh,
Of dreams that linger, passing by.
The heartbeats of the silent trees,
Unravel stories in the breeze.

Moonlight dances on the ground,
Revealing mysteries profound.
Each token hidden in the wood,
Echoes of all that once stood.

From acorns small to mighty oaks,
Life emerges, the earth evokes.
In roots so strong, a legacy,
A tapestry of history.

Listen close, the earth will share,
Of whispered love, of tender care.
In shadows deep, the truth resides,
In roots' embrace, where magic hides.

Twilight's Messenger Amid the Blossom

As twilight calls, the shadows play,
The colors fade from bright to gray.
A hush envelops all around,
In quiet moments, beauty found.

The blossoms sway in gentle breath,
Whispering tales of life and death.
Petals dance beneath the dusk,
Awakening the night's sweet musk.

In twilight's grasp, the secrets bloom,
A fragrant whisper, dispelling gloom.
Softly glowing, fireflies gleam,
On this path, lost in a dream.

The stars peek out, a wink, a cheer,
While twilight's song draws ever near.
In every rustle, every sigh,
The night unfolds, the day says goodbye.

Beneath the sky where shadows blend,
A fleeting moment we must tend.
For twilight's magic, rare and bright,
Woven softly into night.

Crescendo of the Luminous Leaves

In a forest where whispers breathe,
Golden light through branches weaves.
Each leaf a star, in sunlit dance,
Nature's magic, a sweet romance.

Beneath the boughs, shadows play,
Stories told in rustling sway.
A symphony of green so bright,
Guiding dreams through day and night.

Awake, the spirits softly hum,
The ancient pulse, a silent drum.
Every rustle, every sigh,
Nature's secret, a lullaby.

As twilight beckons, colors blend,
Promises kept, the day will mend.
Whispers linger, soft and light,
In harmony, the world ignites.

Crescendo rises, hearts do soar,
In the woods, forevermore.
A tapestry of life's embrace,
In each leaf, a sacred place.

Harmonics of the Lush Understory

Where the ferns and shadows grow,
A silent song begins to flow.
Whispers of life beneath the trees,
Gentle breezes, a soft reprise.

Mossy carpets, emerald dreams,
Twinkling starlight, moonlit beams.
Creatures linger, hidden from view,
In this realm, where magic brews.

Crickets sing a twilight tune,
Sunset drapes the night in bloom.
Petals fall like whispered sighs,
Echoes dance beneath the skies.

In this hush, the heart will find,
A rhythm known to all mankind.
The pulse of earth, both strong and free,
A harmony in mystery.

Here in shadows, secrets weave,
Stories whispered, dusk's reprieve.
Lush and deep, the world does sway,
In the hush of twilight play.

Lifting Veils of the Sylvan Daydream

Morning mist, a silken shroud,
Softly lifting, serene and proud.
Sunbeams break through curtains pale,
Awakening the woodland trail.

With each breeze, a gentle kiss,
Nature's breath in tranquil bliss.
Whispers merge with songs of birds,
In the dawn where magic stirs.

Branches stretch, a welcoming arch,
Guiding paths where dreams may march.
Each moment, a fleeting spark,
Illuminating realms of dark.

Golden rays pierce leafy crowns,
A dance of light where joy abounds.
In this space, where echoes gleam,
Reality meets a vibrant dream.

Veils of sylvan, softly spun,
Cradling secrets from the sun.
In the forest, lost yet found,
Daydreams linger, all around.

Flutter of Wings in the Misty Glade

In the glade where echoes meet,
Butterflies flutter, soft and fleet.
Whispers of color, a vibrant ballet,
Nature's brushstrokes, bright display.

Petals tremble, kissed by air,
Each delicate wing a moment rare.
Life unfurls in graceful arcs,
Delighting hearts, igniting sparks.

Misty veils, the morning's breath,
A canvas soft as silken depth.
Every flutter tells a tale,
Of fleeting dreams on a gentle gale.

Birdsong weaves through leafy seams,
Awakening the hush of dreams.
In the glade where shadows play,
Magic twirls in light's array.

Sweet serenades of wings above,
Lost in the dance of nature's love.
Here in the mist, life takes a stand,
A fleeting touch, a gentle hand.

Whispers of Enchanted Ferns

In moonlit glades where shadows dance,
Beneath the ferns young spirits prance.
With laughter soft as rustling leaves,
They weave a magic that never leaves.

Each whisper held in tender grace,
A fleeting touch, a warm embrace.
The verdant world alive again,
As dreams unfold on emerald fen.

The nightingale sings a sweet refrain,
While secrets linger in the brain.
With every breeze that comes to play,
The ferns keep all the night at bay.

A tapestry of silken green,
In shadows deep, their magic seen.
With every sigh, the forest stirs,
And in its heart, the ferns are hers.

Through tangled roots and starlit beams,
A world of wonder, born of dreams.
Where ancient tales take wing and soar,
The ferns hold echoes of folklore.

Secrets Beneath the Canopy

Beneath the boughs, the stories hum,
Of time forgot, they softly come.
Whispers of old in shadows blend,
Each secret shared, a timeless friend.

Glimmers of light through leaves ascend,
To guide the lost, the wanderer's bend.
A tapestry where magic lies,
In every breath, the forest sighs.

An ancient oak, a guiding hand,
With roots that cradle ancient land.
The murmur of the brook nearby,
A lullaby, a gentle sigh.

The secrets dwell where few may see,
In heart of woods, in bended knee.
Each rustle speaks of dreams once spun,
As twilight falls, the day is done.

In fragrant whispers, night descends,
Embracing all that magic sends.
With each soft breeze, the tales unfurl,
Beneath the green, a hidden world.

Dancers in the Twilight Glade

In twilight's hush, where shadows blend,
The fireflies gather, their dance to send.
In sweet embrace, the fey appear,
With laughter ringing, crystal-clear.

They swirl and spin on dewy grass,
As stars above like diamonds pass.
With twinkling eyes and nimble feet,
They craft a spell, both wild and sweet.

The nightingale calls with notes so pure,
In every heartbeat, magic's cure.
The glade awakens, alive, aglow,
As dreams take flight in silver flow.

With arms stretched wide, the dancers sway,
Under the watch of the moon's soft ray.
The magic lingers, a timeless trance,
In the heart of night, we find our chance.

In every twirl, a wish is made,
In every leap, the fears do fade.
As morning nears, their song resounds,
In twilight's glade, pure joy abounds.

Elfin Echoes of the Verdant Grove

Within the grove where whispers sleep,
The elfin echoes joyfully leap.
In twilight's hue, they weave their song,
A melody sweet, where all belong.

Among the petals, soft and bright,
Their laughter twirls with gentle light.
A dance of joy, both wild and free,
In each soft note, a symphony.

Amidst the trees, a tale unfolds,
Of ancient magic, brave and bold.
With every rustle, secrets sway,
The verdant grove holds night at bay.

In dewdrops shining, dreams are spun,
In each small heartbeat, stories run.
The elfin folk weave dreams so fair,
Their echoes linger on the air.

Beneath the boughs, a world anew,
Where time and space are born in dew.
The joy of nature, pure and true,
In elfin echoes, life shines through.

The Enigma of the Twinkling Thicket

In the heart where shadows play,
A thicket twinkles, bright as day.
Whispers dance on playful breeze,
Secrets rustle through the trees.

Moonlight filters, soft and bright,
Casting dreams in silver light.
Every twinkle tells a tale,
Of wings that flutter, soft and pale.

Creatures small with eyes aglow,
Guide the path where few would go.
Through the thicket, brave souls tread,
Chasing wonders, fears unspread.

Yet beware the thorns that bind,
Not all treasures leave you kind.
For in the glimmering night air,
Lurks a magic, faintly rare.

So venture forth with heart aligned,
In the thicket, truth you'll find.
An enigma wrapped in light,
Calls the seekers of the night.

Enchanted Veils of the Verdant Realm

In the realm where green unfurls,
Veils of enchantment softly swirl.
Nature cloaks her secrets deep,
Guarding dreams in silence, keep.

Lush leaves whisper tales of old,
Mysteries in every fold.
Sunbeams dance on foliage bright,
Painting shadows, pure delight.

Through the glades where fairies play,
Magic weaves in light of day.
Petals blush as breezes sigh,
In this realm, the heart can fly.

Rivers twinkling, laughter sweet,
Echoes of a world complete.
Nature's canvas, vast, sublime,
Holds the rhythm, beats of time.

With every step, a story spun,
In the verdant light of sun.
Here in whispers and in dreams,
Lie the truth of life's bright schemes.

Foliage and Fables at Dusk

As dusk descends, a cloak of dreams,
Fables weave like silver streams.
Leaves rustle soft, a lullaby,
Nature sighs a gentle sigh.

Amidst the trees where shadows creep,
Ancient tales begin to leap.
From fern to oak, each leaf conveys,
Whispers of forgotten days.

In twilight's grip, the world awakes,
Every branch a story makes.
Creatures stir in muted hues,
Mysteries beneath the blues.

The horizon blushes, stars appear,
Glimmering paths that disappear.
Fables echo in the night,
Guiding wanderers with their light.

So pause and listen, hearts attune,
To the songs beneath the moon.
In foliage dense, the truth we seek,
Lies in whispers, soft and sleek.

Melody of the Fairy-Touched Ivy

In corners where the ivy clings,
A melody of magic sings.
Each tendril holds a note so sweet,
Calling hearts on quiet feet.

Green chords strum in gentle air,
Stories spun with utmost care.
Fairy laughter, soft and bright,
Fills the corners of the night.

Dewdrops glisten like the stars,
Whispering truths from afar.
In the dance of leaf and vine,
Lives a song, a tale divine.

With every breeze, a cadence flows,
In the garden, magic grows.
Ivy's touch, a soft embrace,
Guiding souls to hidden space.

So linger here, let worries fade,
In the melody, softly wade.
For in these notes, you're not alone,
In ivy's song, you find your home.

The Gentle Hand of Time's Embrace

In twilight's glow, the shadows play,
With whispers soft, they drift away.
A moment's pause, a fleeting glance,
The heart remembers, caught in a dance.

Beneath the stars, the stories weave,
Of dreams once held, and hopes we leave.
Each ticking clock, a song so sweet,
In every beat, our lives compete.

The river flows, the seasons change,
In time's embrace, we find the strange.
A gentle hand that guides us through,
With every dawn, a path renewed.

Soft as a sigh, the years unfurl,
A tapestry of boy and girl.
The laughter echoes, the tears congeal,
In every memory, a truth revealed.

So dance with time, embrace its flow,
For every moment, we come to know.
A tender gift of life's sweet quest,
In time's embrace, we find our rest.

Ephemeral Grace in the Woodland Slice

In the verdant folds where shadows twist,
Dappled light through the branches kissed.
A fleeting glance at a world so grand,
Where nature's brush strokes softly stand.

The petals fall like whispered lore,
Each breath a tale of meadow's core.
Delicate hues entwined with grace,
In every corner, a sacred space.

A sunbeam's touch on the mossy ground,
Where secrets of the earth abound.
The dance of life, both fierce and fair,
In every rustle, the stories share.

Bright fungi sprout with silly cheer,
While echoes of the past draw near.
An instant's beauty, caught in flight,
A fleeting spark in the soft twilight.

So wander deep where the wild things sigh,
In this ephemeral grace, let your spirit fly.
For in the woods, we find our muse,
In nature's art, we cannot lose.

Reflections on the Surface of the Glade

A mirror lies on the forest floor,
Where every ripple tells of yore.
The wind whispers tales of what has been,
In every shimmer, secrets glean.

The ferns unfurl, their edges bright,
Encapsulating dreams in the fading light.
Barefoot steps on the dampened leaf,
In nature's arms, we find belief.

Clouds drift softly, casting shade,
On tranquil waters, serenity laid.
Each flash of silver, a thought ignites,
In this mosaic of tranquil sights.

A nest of calm where echoes play,
Reflections dance, then fade away.
In every glance, a world distills,
Among the trees, a heart fulfills.

So linger here, let peace invade,
In the quiet depth of the glade.
In nature's mirror, find your grace,
Reflecting gently in this space.

Intricacies of Nature's Gentle Touch

Woven threads in the tapestry bright,
Nature whispers in hues of light.
A spider spins with delicate grace,
Each silken strand, a hand's embrace.

Moss carpets soften each hurried stride,
While whispers of wind through branches glide.
The wildflowers bloom in colors bold,
A story of life in petals told.

Through tangled vines and shadows deep,
The secrets of the forest keep.
With gentle sighs of ancient trees,
The world unfolds with playful ease.

The stream hums low, a soothing sound,
As nature's magic circles round.
Each creature small, each leaf at peace,
In this embrace, we find release.

So let us wander where wonder calls,
In beauty's grasp, our spirit sprawls.
For in the touch of this wild art,
We find the rhythms of the heart.

Fluttering Secrets of the Meadow Realm

In the meadow where wildflowers play,
Secrets flutter as petals sway.
Whispers of magic weave through the air,
Hints of wonders that linger there.

Beneath the sky, a sapphire sea,
Every buzz holds a mystery.
Tiny beings with glimmering wings,
Share their tales like forgotten strings.

Sunbeams dance on the dewdrops bright,
Casting shadows, a flickering light.
Here, the world is filled with glee,
A tapestry of nature's spree.

With every rustle from the grass,
Joyful moments seem to amass.
In the charm of this secret nest,
The heart of magic finds its rest.

As twilight falls, the stars ignite,
Guiding dreams in the quiet night.
Fluttering secrets in every heart,
In the meadow, where dreams depart.

Tangles of Nature's Gentle Tricks

In the thicket where shadows creep,
Nature's magic begins to leap.
Vines entwining, a playful snare,
Tangles dance in the cool, crisp air.

Leaves whisper tales of ages past,
Each rustling sound like a spell cast.
Breezes giggle through branches wide,
A sanctuary where secrets hide.

Sunlight filters through leafy seams,
Painting visions of heartfelt dreams.
Creeping moss holds the earth's embrace,
Nature's gentle tricks, a soft grace.

Where wild things roam, and fairies peak,
In tangled paths, all spirits speak.
The colors blend in a vibrant mix,
Lost in fables of nature's tricks.

As twilight drapes the forest's face,
The stars emerge with a silver lace.
In this realm, mysteries intertwine,
Crafting tales on a verdant line.

A Serenade for Sprightly Greens

Oh, sprightly greens in morning's glow,
Swaying softly, like whispers low.
Fields of emerald, fresh with dew,
A serenade from the earth so true.

Grasshoppers chirp in joyful tune,
Celebrating beneath the moon.
Nature's orchestra, sweet and light,
Plays for creatures that flit in flight.

With every breeze, the poppies dance,
In a swell of colors, a fleeting chance.
Butterflies flutter, a painted breeze,
Lost in the laughter of rustling trees.

Raindrops weave on leafy pearls,
Creating music as life unfurls.
In harmony, the blossoms greet,
A serenade that's pure and sweet.

As daylight wanes, the shadows wane,
In the twilight glow, I hear again.
Sprightly greens in laughter's embrace,
Nature's serenade, a timeless grace.

Fables Born from Woodland Whispers

In woodland realms where silence hums,
Fables grow from the beat of drums.
Each rustle tells of a story spun,
Where ancient hearts and mysteries run.

Trees stand tall, their branches wide,
Guardians of secrets they abide.
Their roots embrace the tales of old,
In twilight's grasp, their legends unfold.

A flicker of light, a shadowed bend,
In every corner, a dream can mend.
Faeries linger with laughter bright,
In the quiet hush, they take their flight.

Under starlit covers, soft and deep,
Whispers linger as the world sleeps.
In every rustling leaf, a song,
A fable where all creatures belong.

With dawn's first light, the magic stirs,
Echoing softly in budding furs.
Fables whispered into the dawn,
In woodland dreams, forever drawn.

The Dance of Faerie Fingers

In twilight's hush, the faeries play,
With fingers like whispers, they sway,
Each twirl a secret, a spell in flight,
Beneath the silver gleam of light.

They weave through shadows, soft and bright,
With laughter that sparkles, pure delight,
Around the flowers, they gently glide,
In a world where magic cannot hide.

Their wings are spun from the dawn's first mist,
With every flicker, a gentle tryst,
In a dance that echoes through the trees,
A sweet, enchanting, whispering breeze.

They gather wishes like dewdrops fair,
And sprinkle them softly, everywhere,
In quiet corners where dreams reside,
With faerie fingers that will not abide.

As night deepens, their glow will dim,
But secrets remain on the moonlit brim,
For in the heart of the gentle night,
The dance of faerie fingers takes flight.

Secrets Woven in Leaf and Light

Amid the trees where shadows creep,
There lie the secrets, soft and deep,
In every leaf, a tale untold,
Of dreams and whispers, brave and bold.

Sunlight dapples the forest floor,
While ancient boughs guard wisdom's lore,
A breeze carries stories from afar,
Wrought from nature's delicate scar.

Threads of gold in the spider's weave,
Entrap the light, the moments we believe,
In hidden glades where silence sways,
And secrets linger in gentle plays.

The dance of shadows among the glen,
Holds the echoes of songs from within,
Every flutter, each rustle, a spark,
Of life unbridled, wild and stark.

In twilight's glow, where magic weaves,
The heart of the forest never leaves,
For secrets bloom in leaf and light,
In the tapestry of the night.

Glimmering Traces of a Wandering Spirit

In fields of dreams, a spirit roams,
Through starlit paths it gently combs,
With glimmering traces in the air,
It whispers secrets, light as prayer.

Each shimmering step a story spun,
Through ferns and flowers, one by one,
A dance of shadows, soft and bright,
In the embrace of the velvet night.

With every sigh, the echoes blend,
Of laughter drifting, a timeless friend,
A wayward song on the breeze of fate,
Calling forth wonders, never too late.

The spirit twirls in twilight's glow,
Leaving behind a radiant show,
In every heart where dreams ignite,
A wandering spirit takes its flight.

In quiet corners, its essence dwells,
Among the stories that time compels,
For fleeting glimpses in the dark,
Reveal the light of a wandering spark.

Echoes of Laughter Among the Ferns

Amidst the ferns where sunlight beams,
The echoes of laughter weave through dreams,
In rustling leaves, a joyful sound,
Where magic breathes and life is found.

The playful whispers of the breeze,
Entwine with giggles that tease and please,
Each fluttering heart in nature's care,
Revealing secrets hidden there.

Beneath the canopy, bright and green,
Life dances lightly, serene and keen,
With every chuckle that softly sways,
The world joins in its merry plays.

The ferns bow low with tales to share,
Of moments cherished, beyond compare,
In a sanctuary where we belong,
The echoes of laughter sing their song.

So pause awhile, let joy reframe,
And in the silence, feel the same,
For laughter lingers, a sweet refrain,
Among the ferns, in sun or rain.

Woven Dreams in the Forest's Heart

In the heart where shadows weave,
Whispers of the past believe.
Moonlight dances on soft moss,
Dreams of old, a gentle gloss.

Branches cradle secrets deep,
Where the ancient spirits sleep.
Fae and sprites in twilight's glow,
Guard the paths where few dare go.

Silver streams reflect the stars,
Guiding souls from places far.
Every rustle tells a tale,
In this forest, lost to pale.

The nightingale sings sweet and low,
To the rhythm of the flow.
Each note, a magic softly spun,
Binding all, beneath the sun.

Through the trees, the soft winds sigh,
Cradling dreams as they flutter by.
In the forest's heart, they gleam,
Woven gently into a dream.

Fluttering Adornments of the Night

In the cloak of night so fine,
Stars like jewels, brightly shine.
Fireflies flicker, weaving light,
Adorning dark with pure delight.

Moonbeams dance on silver streams,
Waking softly all our dreams.
Twirling shadows, spirits flight,
Embrace the magic of the night.

Beneath the boughs, a set of chimes,
Echo soft as whispered rhymes.
Nature's chorus sings so clear,
In every flutter, joy draws near.

The velvet sky, a canvas wide,
Paints the tales that stars confide.
Wings of night, in soft ascent,
Glide through whispers, heaven-sent.

Each moment glimmers with a spark,
In silence deep, a hidden mark.
We dance with dreams, in shadows cast,
A tapestry of night amassed.

Laughter Beneath the Leafy Boughs

In groves where laughter twirls and spins,
Joyful tales of wonder begins.
Children's giggles, bright and free,
Echo through the shady tree.

Beneath the branches, safe and sound,
Magic swirls in whispers found.
Tickling winds, a playful breeze,
Bring forth tales from age-old trees.

Pixies hide in crevices small,
Ready, ever, for a call.
A game of hide and seek they play,
Chasing sunlight through the day.

Their laughter ripples, soft and clear,
Filling hearts with boundless cheer.
As shadows stretch and sunlight fades,
Friendships bloom in perfect shades.

The woods alive with vibrant glee,
A symphony of harmony.
In leafy boughs, our spirits soar,
Laughter cherished, forevermore.

Glints of Light on Sylvan Paths

On sylvan paths where secrets dwell,
Glints of light weave a magic spell.
Each footstep echoes nature's song,
Inviting all who wander along.

Ferns and flowers shimmer bright,
Guiding travelers in soft light.
Whispers of the wind caress,
In this tranquillity, find rest.

Fairy rings and toadstools meet,
Painting lines where forest greets.
Bewitched by dusk, the shadows play,
They dance until the end of day.

Glowing embers of sunset's hue,
Illuminate the path anew.
Rustling leaves share stories grand,
From ancient tales of this enchanted land.

Each glance reveals a world unseen,
Where nature's wonders reign supreme.
So follow softly, let hearts fight,
For in the woods, all souls ignite.

Spirals of Laughter in the Greens

In the glade where laughter twirls,
Among the ferns and dancing pearls.
Children's giggles weave the air,
Sprinkled sunlight, warm and rare.

Mirth that spills like springtime rain,
Filling hearts, dissolving pain.
Whistling breezes join the tune,
As shadows stretch beneath the moon.

Echoes bounce from tree to tree,
In spiral dances, wild and free.
Nature's chorus joins the play,
Our worries banished far away.

Swaying branches hold their breath,
In joyful revel, life, not death.
Every leaf a witness there,
To the magic brewed with care.

So gather near when day is bright,
And let us spin in pure delight.
For in these greens, the world feels right,
Our laughter spins, a wondrous sight.

Earthbound Spirits of the Blossoming Boughs

In quiet nooks where flowers sigh,
The spirits whisper, soft and shy.
Roots entwined with secrets deep,
In blossomed boughs, their wishes keep.

With petals bright as morning sun,
They dance in shadows, one by one.
Tales of love and loss they share,
In fragrant breezes, light as air.

Listen closely, heed the call,
Of earthbound spirits, one and all.
They twirl through time, from bud to bloom,
In every corner, in every room.

Elder trees, with wisdom old,
Guard the dreams and stories told.
In silent reverie, they stand,
An ancient pact with nature's hand.

So wander through the meadows wide,
With open heart and arms spread wide.
Embrace the spirits in their play,
In blossoming boughs, where magic stays.

Floating in Nature's Serenade

As twilight drapes its silken veil,
The world awakens, soft and pale.
A symphony of croaks and notes,
In every leaf, the magic floats.

The brook hums low, a gentle tune,
Reflecting whispers of the moon.
Fireflies dance in twinkling light,
Painting dreams in the soft twilight.

With each soft breeze that brushes by,
The trees sway gently, reaching high.
Nature's melody, warm and bright,
Wraps the night in pure delight.

Songs of crickets rise above,
A serenade, so soft, so love.
In this embrace, the heart can sway,
Floating free as the night turns gray.

So let us linger, breathe it in,
In nature's song, where life begins.
For in this moment, truly free,
We find our place, just you and me.

When Treetops Meet the Dusk

When treetops whisper to the night,
As day recedes and stars take flight.
Their branches stretch with ancient grace,
In twilight's glow, they find their place.

Crickets sing their lullabies,
While shadows dance beneath the skies.
The sky dons robes of purple hue,
As dusk unveils the world anew.

Owl's hoot calls, a solemn friend,
In this stillness, all wounds mend.
Beneath their watchful, watchful eyes,
Dreamers weave their softest sighs.

Golden hues of fading light,
Kiss the leaves, a sweet goodnight.
Nature holds its breath, and then,
In silence deep, we meet again.

So linger here, beneath the trees,
Feel the magic in the breeze.
For when the night begins to fall,
The world awaits our softest call.

Communing with the Flora at Twilight

In twilight's hush, the petals sigh,
A dance of shadows 'neath the sky.
Whispers soft, in colors bold,
Stories of the earth, retold.

The moonbeams weave through leafy lace,
Each flower holds a secret space.
The nightingale sings of lost delight,
Echoes fade in the soft twilight.

The glow of dusk on tangled vines,
A meeting place for ancient signs.
Beneath the stars, the dreams take flight,
As nature's heart beats soft and light.

With every rustle, a voice can be heard,
In each soft sigh, the language of birds.
Nature's canvas, painted in real,
Pulls at the heart, inviting to feel.

So linger here, 'neath the evening's breath,
Where flora whispers, life conquers death.
In the stillness, find your own rhyme,
In the twilight's arms, lose track of time.

Glimmers of Hope within the Tentative Green

Amidst the leaves, a promise stirs,
Bright emerald hues, the world prefers.
Each bud a glimpse of what could be,
A tapestry of hope, wild and free.

Through morning dew, the sunlight beams,
Awakening life from winter's dreams.
Every sprout, a tale begins,
Of courage found and battles won.

In every blade, a story told,
Of seasons passed and hearts so bold.
Tentative green, where shadows play,
Emerging strength, come what may.

And in each rustling, the winds convey,
That through the storms, we'll find our way.
For nature weaves through dark and light,
A glimmer's dance, a guiding sight.

So cherish the blooms, the fragile, the slight,
For within each petal lies a fight.
A hymn of hope, in green we find,
That life and love are intertwined.

Bursts of Wonder in Nature's Palette

In vibrant bursts of colors bright,
Nature paints with sheer delight.
Upon the canvas of the day,
Every hue has much to say.

With strokes of gold and strokes of blue,
The meadow whispers, fresh and new.
The brushes dance, the swirls are grand,
Life's artistry at nature's hand.

Each blossom nods, a part of the scene,
In quiet grace, their voices keen.
Petals soft like whispers blend,
In their embrace, all hearts amend.

From hilltops high to valleys low,
The colors flow, a vibrant show.
With every step on dewy grass,
Breathe in the visions as you pass.

So lose yourself in nature's art,
Let it awaken your own heart.
In every corner, marvel, behold,
The bursts of wonder, stories told.

Meadow Dreams in the Heart of Glimmer

In meadows wide, where wildflowers swayed,
A tapestry of dreams arrayed.
Soft whispers breeze through golden stalks,
As lives unfold in carefree walks.

Each blade of grass tells tales of old,
Of summers kissed and winters cold.
With every flutter, the meadow breathes,
In tender hues, the spirit weaves.

With sunlight dappling through the leaves,
In nature's grip, the heart believes.
Where laughter dances on the air,
And whispers linger everywhere.

The gentle hum of bumblebee,
Awakens the dreams that long to be.
Between the petals, secrets lay,
In the glow of dusk, they find their way.

So rest awhile, let spirits soar,
In meadow dreams, you'll find much more.
In every shadow, in each gleam,
Life's enchantment blooms, it's all a dream.

The Hidden Realm of Evergreen Whimsy

In a forest dense with dreams,
Whispers dance on gentle beams,
Mossy carpets softly sway,
Where the lost and fairies play.

Glimmers weave through ancient trees,
Carried forth by playful breeze,
Hidden paths of emerald hue,
Lead to magic, pure and true.

Underneath the twilight's glow,
Secrets hidden, yet they flow,
Harmonies of laughter bright,
Echo softly through the night.

Every shadow casts a tale,
Of the brave who dared to sail,
Through this realm of endless dreams,
Where enchantment softly gleams.

With a charm that captures hearts,
In this world, where wonder starts,
Come, dear friend, take a chance,
Join the forest's timeless dance.

Moonlit Prowl through Twisting Vines

When the moonlight starts to creep,
Through the leaves, where secrets sleep,
Stars above twinkle so bright,
Guiding shadows through the night.

Vines entwined like whispered lore,
Tugging softly at the core,
Where the wild things softly sigh,
And the nightingale's sweet cry.

Step with care on silvery paths,
Feel the magic that it hath,
Every rustle, every cheek,
Nature's voice begins to speak.

Underneath the fruit-laden boughs,
Eyes aglow as the moon bows,
Creatures gather for the feast,
In this night, we are released.

So let the night weave its charm,
Wrap your heart in gentle balm,
In this dance of vine and light,
Find your spirit, take to flight.

Nature's Dialogue with the Spirit World

Listen close to nature's breath,
In the stillness, beyond death,
Leaves converse with ancient souls,
Whispering of forgotten roles.

Wind carries tales of the past,
Through the twilight dim and vast,
Every rustle, every sigh,
Echoes softly, never die.

In the silent woods of grace,
Ghostly forms begin to trace,
Patterns knit by hand unseen,
Nature's weave, the in-between.

Fingers touch the ethereal,
In this realm, so surreal,
A dialogue beyond the norm,
Where spirits linger, bright and warm.

So walk with care, and greet the dusk,
For in shadows, there's magic's trust,
And in every gentle breeze,
Live the dreams of ancient trees.

The Enchantment of Shimmering Twigs

In the hush of twilight's call,
Shimmering twigs, they rise and fall,
Glimmers caught in evening's kiss,
Nature's jewels, none can miss.

Dancing shadows, soft and light,
Spin a tale upon the night,
With each twig, a story spun,
Of moonlit lands and all that's fun.

Listen closely, hear them sing,
Tales of joy and sorrow bring,
Woven in with starry threads,
Where the magic gently spreads.

Every crackle, each soft snap,
Holds a legend in its trap,
Come and delve in what you find,
A world where you leave woes behind.

Beneath the arch of sighing trees,
Feel the balm of evening breeze,
In this grove of twigs aglow,
Let your heart and spirit grow.

Shadows of Moss-Kissed Starlight

In silken night where whispers weave,
The shadows dance, the stars deceive.
Moonbeams waltz on velvet streams,
Awake the world with wistful dreams.

Ancient roots in quiet lore,
Guard secrets held for hearts to score.
Each breath a song, each glance a tale,
Where magic blooms, the brave prevail.

Beneath the boughs where echoes sigh,
The owls observe, the willows cry.
A tapestry of softest light,
Crochets the realm of dreams ignited.

Yet in the dark, a hush does fall,
As shadows stretch against the wall.
Their emerald cloak, a mystic shroud,
Embraces wishes, soft yet loud.

For in the moss where starlight gleams,
Hope lingers long in woven dreams.
Each tiny spark, a heart reborn,
In shadows cast when night is worn.

Sprouts of Magic in the Moonlit Haze

In fields aglow with silvery mist,
Young sprouts awaken, a forgotten tryst.
With whispered spells and laughter light,
They twirl in circles, a graceful sight.

The moon, a witness to playful schemes,
Enfolds the earth with tender beams.
Every blossom raises its head,
To greet the stars where wishes are fed.

Night-breezes carry secrets sweet,
As fairies frolic on tiny feet.
In every heart, a spark ignites,
In darkness found, true magic sights.

Through shadows thick and twilight deep,
The dreams that in the forest seep.
Become the tales of ages past,
In moonlit haze, where shadows cast.

With each soft sigh, new wonders bloom,
Elixirs brewed in nature's room.
The night enfolds, with gentle grace,
As magic sprouts in moonlight's embrace.

Woodland Folly of Glimmering Petals

In woodland depths where colors blend,
The petals shine, their beauty lends.
A folly crafted by nature's hand,
Where dreams and flowers sweep the land.

Each fragrant hue, a story told,
Of love and laughter, brave and bold.
The glimmering shades, they sway in tune,
With every whisper of the moon.

Beneath the branches, secrets nest,
In twilight shadows, they find rest.
Gentle creatures in silence play,
As time weaves gold through night and day.

The forest hums a melody sweet,
With rustling leaves and dancing feet.
A symphony of life reborn,
In petals bright by dew adorned.

So wander through this floral maze,
Where every turn leads to a gaze.
At woodland folly, dreams take flight,
In glimmering petals kissed by night.

A Chorus of Hidden Thorns

In tangled vines, where shadows creep,
A chorus sings, through night they leap.
The thorns, they guard what lies within,
A beauty veiled, where dreams begin.

When twilight cloaks the world in gray,
A symphony of whispers play.
Each note of heartache, joy entwined,
In secret songs of nature lined.

Among the brambles, courage grows,
From deepest sorrows, strength thus flows.
The hidden truths, like roses bloom,
In fragrant air, dispel the gloom.

Though sharp the pricks that guard the way,
In every wound, a story lay.
A dancer twirls in thorny grace,
In shadows cast, find your own place.

So heed the voice of thorns concealed,\nFor struggles
faced can be revealed.
In harmony, life's lessons learn,
A chorus sung through hidden thorns.

The Enchanted Sunshine's Expression

Golden beams through leaves do play,
Whispering secrets of the day.
Each ray a blessing, warmth bestowed,
On hearts where dreams and hopes explode.

As laughter mingles with the light,
The world awakens, pure delight.
Illuminated paths unfold,
A tapestry of joy, pure gold.

With every dawn, the magic wakes,
In hues of amber, love it makes.
The skies aglow with wishes bright,
A spellbound dance of day and night.

In gentle gardens, shadows twirl,
Where sunlight's fingers softly unfurl.
With every flutter, nature sighs,
In symphonies of warms and highs.

The enchanted sunshine's embrace,
Brings forth a smile, a warm grace.
In every heart, this magic lives,
In every moment, love it gives.

Shimmers Found in Leafy Cradles

Within the grove, where whispers dwell,
Shimmers twinkle, cast a spell.
Each leaf a cradle, green and bright,
Hiding treasures in the light.

Beneath the branches, dreams take flight,
In cool shadows, a dance of light.
A symphony of rustling grace,
Nature's jewels, they interlace.

The dew has kissed each emerald face,
In shimmering silence, time leaves its trace.
A world awakened, softly spun,
As golden moments come undone.

With every breeze, the laughter stirs,
Among the ferns, in distant purrs.
In leafy cradles, magic grows,
In peaceful dreams, where wonder flows.

Oh, shimmers found in gentle beams,
In every nook, where nature dreams.
Embrace the quiet, close your eyes,
For in this world, the magic lies.

The Dance of Petals at Dawn

At dawn, when the world's still asleep,
The petals rise from slumber deep.
In hues of pink and violet dreams,
They sway gently, or so it seems.

A ballet of grace in morning air,
As light filters through, pure and fair.
With every breeze, a soft caress,
In floral tune, they whirl and bless.

The garden awakens, colors ignite,
As petals twirl in morning light.
A whispered tune that nature sings,
The joy that every sunrise brings.

Soft fragrances dance, so divine,
Each blossom's secret, a hidden line.
In rhythmic movements, tender embrace,
The petals' dance is full of grace.

Oh, join the chorus, let your spirit soar,
In the dance of petals, forevermore.
As dawn unfolds, let your heart be free,
In nature's beauty, find your glee.

Roots of Enchantment in the Forest

Deep in the woods where magic grows,
Roots intertwine, as ancient prose.
With whispers soft beneath the ground,
In earthy tales, all wisdom found.

Each twisted branch, each gnarled tree,
Holds stories cloaked in mystery.
A sanctuary, a hidden lore,
Where spirits linger, forevermore.

The canopy weaves a sheltering shade,
In dappled light, enchantments laid.
With every step, a secret calls,
In the heart of the forest, magic falls.

From roots to sky, the cycle spins,
In every heartbeat, the forest wins.
A living tapestry, woven tight,
Where every shadow dances in light.

Oh, find the roots of enchantment there,
In whispered breezes, in the air.
For in the forest, dreams take flight,
In every corner, pure delight.

Flickering Lights Beneath the Canopy

Beneath the leaves where shadows play,
Small lights flicker, dance, and sway.
Whispers echo in the night,
As stars peek through the fading light.

A gentle breeze begins to weave,
Tales of magic to believe.
In hidden nooks, the fireflies gleam,
Lighting paths where dreamers dream.

The ancient trees in silence stand,
Guardians of this enchanted land.
With secrets held in every bark,
The night awakens with a spark.

Mysterious calls from far and wide,
Guide the wanderers who abide.
They seek the truth in nature's art,
And find the song within their heart.

As dawn approaches, all will fade,
Yet memories of the night cascade.
Flickering lights beneath the trees,
Whisper tales carried by the breeze.

Elfin Laughter in the Breeze

In meadows bright, where wildflowers grow,
Elfin laughter dances to and fro.
With every giggle, joy does sprout,
Magic mingles, casting doubt.

The sunbeams glisten on dewdrops fair,
As gossamer wings float through the air.
A celebration of light and cheer,
Echoing laughter, soft yet clear.

Underneath the willow's sway,
Elves gather 'round at close of day.
With twinkling eyes and hearts so bold,
They weave a story yet untold.

Secrets whispered on the breeze,
A sprinkle of laughter with such ease.
They dance through shadows, bright and fast,
In a world where dreams are unsurpassed.

And though the night will come too soon,
Elfin laughter hums a tune.
A melody carried, sweet and light,
In every heart, a spark ignites.

Secrets of the Verdant Grove

In the heart of the grove, where the wild things play,
Secrets are hidden in the mossy array.
Leaves rustle softly, a mystic tune,
Guarding the wisdom of sun and moon.

Ancient boughs twist and curl with care,
Breath of the forest fills the air.
Curious whispers weave through the trees,
Telling the stories of ages past ease.

A hidden path where few dare tread,
Leads to the places where magic is fed.
With every step, the light grows dim,
Shadows dance on a whispered whim.

From acorn to oak, each life entwined,
The grove holds the secrets that fate has designed.
In the rustle of leaves, you can hear the song,
Of all that was right, and all that was wrong.

So seek the heart of the verdant shade,
Where nature's wonders are gently laid.
For in those echoes, you'll find the key,
To unlock the secrets of all that could be.

Gossamer Threads of Nature's Spell

In the dawn's embrace, where shadows play,
Gossamer threads weave night into day.
Softly they shimmer, in colors bright,
Creating a tapestry of pure delight.

With every whisper of the wind's plea,
Nature reveals her mystery.
Patterns emerge, so delicate, rare,
A dance in the air, a breath of fresh air.

A tapestry spun of sun and dew,
Threads of the earth, both ancient and new.
The flowers sway, their colors unfurl,
In the heart of the woods, a magical whirl.

In twilight's glow, the threads entwine,
Nature's fingers, both gentle and fine.
Holding the dreams of the earth and the sky,
Crafting a world where wishes can fly.

So pause for a moment, breathe in the spell,
Feel the magic, let your heart swell.
For in nature's embrace, we find our way,
In gossamer threads, we're never astray.

A Symphony of Sprouts and Spirits

In dawn's embrace, the blossoms sing,
Soft whispers carried on the breeze.
A world alive with vibrant spring,
Where magic thrives among the trees.

The woodland dances, shadows play,
Each leaf a note in nature's score.
The spirit of the earth's ballet,
Invites us to explore much more.

Beneath the boughs of tall, stout oaks,
The laughter of the brook is clear.
In every glade, a tale provokes,
A symphony for hearts to hear.

Glowworms flicker in twilight's gaze,
The stars awash in soft, sweet light.
As dusk adorns the forest's phase,
A realm where day gives way to night.

Amidst the sprouts, bright spirits sigh,
Their laughter lingers on the air.
In nature's arms, we long to fly,
A harmony beyond compare.

Elusive Echoes of the Enchanted Wood

In shadows deep, the whispers flow,
Each echo holds a tale untold.
The forest guards its secrets low,
Where dreams and memories unfold.

A path adorned with silver light,
Inviting footsteps, soft and slow.
Through tangled roots, both day and night,
The magic of the wood will show.

In twilight's glow, the faeries dance,
With laughter weaving through the trees.
They spin a spell, a fleeting chance,
To glimpse the heart of mysteries.

The brook sings songs of ancient lore,
While winds carry the secrets near.
Each rustling leaf, a whispered score,
Reminds us why we linger here.

Elusive echoes call our name,
In realms where gentle spirits tread.
We seek the spark, the hidden flame,
Among the paths where few have fled.

Winding Paths of Sylvan Dreams

In tangled woods where shadows weave,
The winding paths lead hearts astray.
With every step, we dare believe,
That magic waits at close of day.

A canopy of emerald hues,
Above, the branches twist and twine.
In hidden glades, we chase the muse,
As whispers through the twilight shine.

With every rustle calls a spark,
Of inspiration bright and new.
The forest breathes, both light and dark,
Where dreams and stories intertwine too.

Each flower blooms, a promise made,
In colors rich as heart's delight.
The gentle touch of morning's shade,
Awakens joy within the night.

On winding paths, our souls take flight,
In search of wonders pure and true.
For in the woods, both day and night,
A symphony of dreams imbue.

The Gentle Caress of Forest Air

A breezy touch among the pines,
Where every sigh ignites the soul.
The gentle air through branches twines,
In woodland realms, we find our whole.

Beneath the boughs, the whispers glide,
Each rustling leaf, a soft caress.
The earth's embrace, where dreams abide,
In nature's arms, we find our rest.

The fragrant blooms, a fragrant song,
Of blossoms burst in vibrant light.
Each moment here, where we belong,
A refuge from the world's great plight.

The softest hush, the sweetest sound,
The forest cradles every care.
In every breath, enchantment found,
A journey forged in forest air.

As day converts to cool night's sway,
The stars emerge, a soft cloak spun.
In every shade, we lose our way,
And yet, we find the truest fun.

Flickers of Joy among the Twisting Vines

In twilight's grasp, the shadows sway,
Delighting hearts in a dance at play.
Each laughter sings through tangled leaves,
A chorus born where magic weaves.

With every flicker, hope ignites,
A spark that sails through moonlit nights.
In quiet corners, whispers bloom,
Beneath the stars, dispelling gloom.

Amongst the vines, the dreams entwine,
A tapestry of fate divine.
In every sigh, a story spun,
Beneath the gaze of a watchful sun.

In labyrinths of green we find,
The secrets held, the ties that bind.
Flickers of joy entwined with fate,
A dance that sings of love innate.

So wander deep where shadows cling,
Amidst the vines, your spirit sing.
For in the dark, the light will gleam,
And whisper softly of our dream.

Fairies in the Dew-kissed Garden

In dawn's embrace, the glimmers play,
With fluttering wings at break of day.
Among the blooms, they laugh and twirl,
Their sparkling dust, a gentle whirl.

The petals bow as soft winds sigh,
While fairies dance beneath the sky.
With every step, a tale unfolds,
In dewy realms where magic holds.

Bright colors bloom in warmth and light,
A tapestry of pure delight.
In each soft breeze, their voices sing,
Of whispered hopes that mornings bring.

Where flowers meet the sunlit hue,
The fairies weave a world so true.
They mirror dreams in shimmering dew,
And paint the skies in shades anew.

So wander there with open heart,
In gardens where the soul takes part.
For every flower, a secret bears,
And fairies dance amidst our cares.

Songs of the Rustling Ferns

In shadows deep, where ferns unfold,
Their whispers tell of tales retold.
Soft rustlings breathe of ages past,
In nature's arms, our anchors cast.

As breezes weave through emerald fronds,
The forest hums with ancient bonds.
Each note a promise, sweet and clear,
A melody that draws us near.

Through dappled light, their secrets bask,
In every shade, a hidden task.
With every sway, the stories call,
A symphony amidst the thrall.

In tranquil spaces, calm and deep,
The songs of ferns invite our sleep.
They guard the dreams of earth and sky,
On gentle wings, our spirits fly.

So listen close, and you may find,
The rustling ferns, they speak, they bind.
In verdant realms where echoes play,
Their songs will guide you on your way.

The Artistry of the Verdant Amulet

Amidst the trees where shadows weave,
A verdant amulet weaves to believe.
Crafted from leaves in emerald hues,
A treasure born of nature's muse.

Each branch adorned with silken lace,
In sunlight's glow, a warm embrace.
Within its core, the stories dwell,
Of ancient woods and all they tell.

The artistry of life strikes true,
In whispers soft as morning dew.
With every pulse, the magic flows,
In every heart, the wonder grows.

From roots that anchor to skies that soar,
The amulet holds the earth at its core.
Binding realms with gentle grace,
A timeless dance in nature's space.

So wear this charm, and let it sing,
Of hidden paths and wondrous things.
For in your heart, its beauty stays,
A verdant amulet, love's embrace.

Whispers of Woodland Shadows

In the heart of the wood where spirits dwell,
Secrets ride on the breeze, they softly tell.
Fingers of vines weave a tapestry grand,
While shadows dance gently, guided by hand.

Moonlight glimmers on leaves of jade,
Hushed whispers echo in the cool evening shade.
Dreams intertwine with the rustling leaves,
Nature's own magic, for those who believe.

Footsteps tread lightly on soft, mossy ground,
Awakened are creatures, mysterious and profound.
Each rustle and sigh holds a tale yet untold,
In the whispers of shadows, enchantment unfolds.

Glimmers of starlight cradle the night,
While faeries and flickers play in the light.
The beckoning woods call with a soft, sweet hum,
Inviting the dreamers, their hearts will succumb.

Here in this haven where magic is real,
Every breath taken holds the charm of a reel.
In whispers of woodland, together we roam,
Finding our solace, a wild, wondrous home.

Dancing Leaves in Twilight

As daylight dimmers to a soft, glowing hue,
Leaves twirl and flutter, like butterflies too.
They whisper sweet songs of the day now gone,
In twilight's embrace, a new dance is drawn.

Branches sway gently, a rhythm divine,
Beneath the blush sky, where the stars intertwine.
Nature is clad in an evening's attire,
The cool air ignites a playful desire.

The rust-colored maples, they spin and they sway,
Catching the dreams that softly drift away.
Every gust carries a tale from above,
As leaves whisper secrets and stories of love.

Crickets begin their soft serenade,
A chorus of life in the twilight parade.
The world grows still, as the night takes its claim,
In dancing leaves' laughter, we whisper your name.

With shadows extending like curtains unfurl,
The magic of twilight begins to unfurl.
Holding hands with the night, we sway to the tune,
In the dance of the leaves, beneath the soft moon.

The Sprightly Green Enchantment

Amidst the lush glades where wildflowers bloom,
Their colors burst forth, dispelling all gloom.
The sun paints the meadows in bright golden hues,
While laughter of fairies drifts softly like dew.

Beneath the tall oaks, their branches like arms,
The earth sings a lullaby, nature's own charms.
In pockets of sunlight, the soft shadows play,
Inviting the wanderers to linger and stay.

Breezes carry giggles through each emerald glade,
Where sunlight dapples the paths that we've made.
With every small movement, whispers arise,
In the sprightly enchantment, our spirits will rise.

The flutter of wings and the whisper of leaves,
Where secrets of nature are softly conceived.
Every glint of the light holds a story so bright,
In the heart of the green, oh, what pure delight!

In this woodland wonder, we'll frolic and twirl,
In the sprightly embrace of this magical world.
A tapestry woven with laughter and song,
Forever enchanted, where hearts truly belong.

Mystical Tendrils of the Glen

In the glen where the wildflowers twine and weave,
Mystical tendrils beckon, daring us to believe.
With each breath of wind, a new wonder unfolds,
A tapestry woven with shimmering golds.

Echoes of laughter skate on the breeze,
As secrets emerge from the heart of the trees.
With whispers of magic that swirl all around,
We dance in the twilight to the soft, soothing sound.

Through hollows and arches, where mysteries dwell,
At the heart of the glen, there's a potent spell.
Roots grasp the earth in an ancient embrace,
In this enchanted sanctuary, we find our place.

Dreamcatchers woven from the night's gentle sigh,
Capture the stars as they twinkle up high.
Where wishes are carried on the frail autumn air,
The glen holds its secrets for those who will dare.

So wander with me, through the shadows and light,
In the mystical glen, everything feels right.
Together we'll journey where dreams intertwine,
In the tendrils of magic, our spirits align.

Frolic of the Diminutive Sprouts

In sunlit glades where shadows play,
The diminutive sprouts dance and sway.
With laughter sweet, they twirl around,
In every nook, joy can be found.

Tiny feet on dew-kissed leaves,
Whispered secrets, nature weaves.
A world so small yet oh so grand,
Together they thrive, hand in hand.

Petal hats and leafy cloaks,
They sing of life with joyous yokes.
With each soft giggle, spirits rise,
The heart of earth beneath the skies.

In twilight's glow, they leap and spring,
A melody the night can bring.
The stars lean down to join their spree,
A frolic shared with reverie.

So let them dance in wild delight,
The diminutive sprouts, a wondrous sight.
With every heartbeat, every cheer,
They paint the world with magic here.

Singing Breezes in Gossamer Threads

Through emerald fields where whispers soar,
The breezes sing, a timeless lore.
In gossamer threads, they weave a song,
Entwining hearts, where dreams belong.

Soft caresses brush against the face,
As if the air knew its own place.
With every note, the world transforms,
In nature's choir, the spirit warms.

Gliding past, the whispers play,
A symphony that lights the day.
In laughter carried, peace does thread,
The magic of what's often said.

Windswept tales of love and care,
In every breeze, a secret air.
They dance through branches, swift and free,
Binding earth and sky in harmony.

As twilight invites a hush profound,
The singing breezes gather around.
With every heart, the threads entwine,
In gentle rhythm, they divine.

Revelry of the Celestial Canopy

Beneath the sky, a vast display,
The celestial canopy leads the way.
Stars like lanterns twinkle bright,
Guiding dreams through the velvety night.

In hushed whispers, the cosmos gleams,
As earthbound souls embrace their dreams.
With silver light, the moon ascends,
A radiant glow that never ends.

Galaxies swirl in playful dance,
Each shooting star, a fleeting chance.
In cosmic revelry, hearts align,
Across the universe, destinies twine.

Clouds drift softly, a tender shroud,
Holding secrets of the dreaming crowd.
In harmony, they weave and spin,
Unity born from deep within.

So let us bask in this great expanse,
Embrace the wonder, join the dance.
In the revelry of night's embrace,
We find our place in timeless space.

Light-Hearted Explorations in the Glade

In verdant nooks where pathways weave,
Light-hearted souls dare to believe.
With every step, a new delight,
Explorations spark beneath the light.

They chase the sun through dappled trees,
With laughter mingling in the breeze.
In whispered tales of wood and glen,
Adventure calls again and again.

Curious minds with sparkling eyes,
They seek the wonder 'neath the skies.
Each stone unturned, each flower found,
Reveals the magic that does abound.

With nature's palette, colors blaze,
In vibrant hues, their spirits raise.
With hearts unburdened, free to roam,
In every journey, they find home.

So join the frolic, leave behind,
The weight of worries, free the mind.
In light-hearted explorations, see,
The beauty of the glade set free.

Playful Greenery in Twilight's Embrace

In whispers soft, the leaves do play,
As twilight dances, fading day.
The branches sway, a gentle song,
Where shadows flicker, dreams belong.

With emerald hues that glint and gleam,
The world awakes from day's sweet dream.
A flutter here, a rustle there,
In evening's charm, we find our lair.

The flowers bloom, their colors bright,
Beneath the stars, a wondrous sight.
The breeze, it carries secrets old,
In twilight's arms, the tales unfold.

As crickets sing a lullaby,
The moon ascends the velvet sky.
In playful greenery, we roam,
In twilight's embrace, we find our home.

With laughter light, we chase the night,
In the garden's heart, pure delight.
A world enchanted, soft and slow,
In twilight's arms, we bloom and grow.

Tales from the Hidden Hollow

In a hollow deep where shadows dwell,
The stories weave a magic spell.
With every tree, a whisper sighs,
Of dreams long past, beneath the skies.

The brook hums low a secret song,
Where creatures pause to sing along.
The twilight glimmers, soft and fine,
In each dark nook, tales intertwine.

The foxes prance on velvet paws,
As owls declare the night's applause.
In hidden corners, wonders sprout,
With every flicker, dreams break out.

The ancient oaks stand tall and grand,
Guardians of the stories planned.
In whispered tones, the past returns,
As time within this hollow churns.

Beneath the stars, the echoes play,
In harmony, they drift away.
In every leaf, a legend sprout,
In hidden hollow, dreams take route.

Enchantment Beneath the Arching Boughs

Beneath the boughs, where shadows fall,
An enchantment whispers, beckons all.
With every leaf, a tale is spun,
A tapestry of moonlit fun.

The fireflies drift, a sparkling dance,
In twilight's glow, they take their chance.
Each fluttering light, a wishful sigh,
In the embrace of the evening sky.

The soft, cool grass invites a pause,
As nature plays its gentle cause.
Among the roots, the secrets play,
In arching boughs, where midnight sways.

The stars lean down, the night unfolds,
With stories rich, and magic bold.
In every corner, wonders weave,
In the dark depths, we dare believe.

So linger here, as dreams take flight,
In hidden realms of softest night.
In nature's heart, our spirits soar,
Beneath the boughs, forever more.

Chasing Fireflies in the Twilight Mist

In twilight's soft and misty glow,
We chase the fireflies, high and low.
Their lanterns wink, a playful tease,
As we dance through the whispering trees.

With every step, a spark ignites,
In a world adorned with magic lights.
The air is sweet, the laughter bright,
As shadows twirl in the fading light.

The moon peeks in, a silvery smile,
Guiding our hearts for a little while.
With every flicker, we're drawn near,
To nature's magic, so precious and clear.

Through dewy grass and gentle sighs,
We weave our dreams beneath the skies.
In every flash, the night unfolds,
A canvas painted in tales and gold.

So let us bask in evening's kiss,
With fireflies lighting the night's abyss.
In twilight mist, our spirits fly,
Chasing the wonders, we can't deny.

Echoes of the Forgotten Glen

In the glen where shadows play,
Whispers of time drift away.
Mossy stones and trees so old,
Secrets of stories yet untold.

Beneath the boughs of ancient oak,
Gentle laughter, a vanished joke.
Moonlit paths where fairies danced,
Echoes linger, dreams entranced.

Rivers hum a soft refrain,
Carrying tales through sun and rain.
Silent glimmers on the stream,
Nurtured by a wistful dream.

In twilight's clutch, the breezes sigh,
Guarding truths that soar and fly.
Among the ferns, the past remains,
Threads of magic in the veins.

A place where hope and sorrow blend,
In every heart, a longing penned.
The glen remembers those who roam,
In whispers, claiming them as home.

Hidden Pathways through the Fading Light

Winding trails in dusky glow,
Lead to places few can know.
Petals fall like whispered dreams,
Carried on the evening streams.

Gone the sun, the world transforms,
Silhouettes in gentle swarms.
A lantern's flicker, shadows chase,
Fleeting glimpses of a face.

The wild paths, a secret bind,
Where tangled roots tend to unwind.
Crickets chant, a soft refrain,
Nature's pulse, a steady gain.

Dappled light through leaves above,
Kisses paths with gentle love.
Each step taken, magic grows,
Unravelling the hidden prose.

Fleeting moments linger here,
Lost in time but ever near.
Haunting echoes wrap the night,
Guiding souls through fading light.

Trysts in the Dappled Shade

Underneath the leafy dome,
Hearts entwined, they find their home.
Sunbeams dance on skin so fair,
In the sanctuary of the air.

Breezes whisper, laughter rings,
Lovers bound by hidden things.
Secrets shared with every glance,
In the shade, they weave their chance.

Gentle sighs and stolen looks,
The world just fades like open books.
A tapestry of fleeting time,
Embroidered softly, pure and prime.

Here where roots entwine and grow,
Love's sweet nectar starts to flow.
Against the bark, a promise made,
Within the shade, their dreams cascade.

Moments linger, held so tight,
In dappled shade, a spark ignites.
Hearts ablaze, they brave the day,
Blissful trysts in love's array.

Paintings of Twilight Among the Roots

Strokes of lavender paint the sky,
As day gives way with a gentle sigh.
Roots embrace the earth below,
Holding stories, rich and slow.

In twilight's grasp, the colors blend,
Canvas stretched, paths that wend.
Violet hues and shadows creep,
Inviting dreamers into sleep.

Hushed whispers in the cool night air,
Brush of ghosts, a fleeting flare.
Stars awaken, shimmering bright,
Marking journeys lost to sight.

The earth adorned with tales of time,
Brushstrokes rich with reason and rhyme.
Each root a tale in silence told,
Of dreams that dared to be bold.

With every sunset, new worlds spark,
Painting legends in the dark.
Twilight's art, a moment rare,
In deep-rooted dreams, we share.

The Faery's Caress in the Green

In twilight's hush, the faery flits,
With silver wings, a soft embrace.
Among the flowers, moonlight sits,
Her laughter spills, a gentle grace.

The leaves do dance, in breezes light,
A symphony of whispered dreams.
Through shimmering soft glow of night,
A magic weaves in silver streams.

Each petal sways, a subtle sigh,
As glimmers sparkle in the air.
With every heart, she draws us nigh,
To secrets held, beyond compare.

Her touch is warmth, the chill subsides,
A tapestry of life unfolds.
In nature's arms, our spirit glides,
A tale of love that ne'er grows old.

So linger here, in verdant dreams,
Where faery whispers heal the heart.
The world is more than what it seems,
In every shade, she plays her part.

Wistful Boughs in the Misty Whisper

Beneath the boughs where shadows meld,
The mist does weave its quiet song.
In whispers deep, the secrets held,
The heart finds where it feels belong.

The branches sway, like dancers bold,
Alluring tales in silence told.
Each rustle lures with mystery,
Of ages past, of history.

A glimmer shines through twilight's veil,
As time stands still in nature's hold.
With every breath, both soft and frail,
The echoes stir of stories old.

In every leaf a wish is cast,
As dreams take root in sacred ground.
The present fades, the future's vast,
In wistful boughs, we are spellbound.

So linger here, where moments wane,
Amid the mist, our souls take flight.
In whispers soft, we find our gain,
In nature's grace, a pure delight.

Tendrils of Creation Dancing

In twilight's glow, the tendrils twine,
A tapestry of life and light.
Through every breath, the dreams align,
In colors bold, both dark and bright.

The petals open, softly sway,
A dance of life, a sweet embrace.
With every dawn, the shadows play,
Creation's art, a fleeting trace.

The whispers of the earth unite,
In fertile soil, new dreams take root.
Each tendril spirals, pure delight,
In rhythms born from nature's flute.

In gentle winds, the stories flow,
Our lives entwined, like roots below.
With every heartbeat, change is near,
The dance of life, both bright and clear.

So let us weave, with hands and heart,
A narrative of light and shade.
In every stroke, we play our part,
In tendrils of creation laid.

Secrets in the Greenhouse of Dreams

Within the walls of glass and light,
A greenhouse holds both hopes and fears.
Where dreams take root in tender night,
And every tear is sown with years.

The blossoms pulse with vibrant hues,
Each petal sings a tale untold.
In fragrant air, the essence stews,
Of light and dark, both young and old.

The whispers swirl, a hidden grace,
As ivy climbs with gentle care.
In silence finds a sacred space,
Where secrets linger in the air.

With every touch, the magic blooms,
A vivid world, unseen, unknown.
To wander here is to consume,
The wonders that in shadows groan.

So enter in, let heart take flight,
Among the dreams where wishes gleam.
In secrets kept, both day and night,
A sacred dance begins to dream.

Charm of the Blossomed Trails

In the garden where dreams take flight,
Petals dance in morning's light.
Colors bright, like stars above,
Whisper secrets of summer's love.

Every path where blossoms bloom,
Echoes soft with nature's tune.
Joy resides in every glance,
As fragrances weave a gentle dance.

Breezes carry tales of old,
Stories waiting to be told.
With each step upon the ground,
Magic lingers all around.

Underneath the azure sky,
Wanderers pause and softly sigh.
The charm of trails that twist and wind,
Leads to treasures we shall find.

So let us roam with hearts so free,
Where blossoms hold the key to glee.
In every petal, a soft embrace,
The charm of trails, our sacred space.

The Twine of Nature's Embrace

In hidden glades where shadows play,
Twining roots weave night and day.
Nature's fingers softly link,
In whispered dreams, we pause and think.

The melody of rustling leaves,
A symphony that never grieves.
Gentle streams weave through the glen,
Carving paths where joy begins.

Sunlight dapples through the trees,
A playful dance upon the breeze.
Every whisper, every sigh,
Makes the heart leap, makes it fly.

In fields where wildflowers sway,
Love blooms bright and brightens day.
Nature's arms, a warm embrace,
Inviting us to find our place.

So gather 'round, let laughter bring,
The twine of joy that nature sings.
Between the branches, dreams shall trace,
In every heart, nature's grace.

Lullabies of the Whispering Pines

Beneath the boughs where secrets hide,
Lullabies of comfort glide.
Pines stand tall, with stories grand,
Guardians of this enchanted land.

Gentle winds hum soft and low,
Carrying tales of long ago.
In their embrace, worries wane,
As tranquility flows like rain.

Moonlight filters through the trees,
Casting dreams upon the breeze.
Nature hums a soothing song,
Where weary hearts can drift along.

Stars above twinkle and glance,
Inviting souls into a trance.
The night unfolds, a magic sign,
In lullabies of whispering pines.

So close your eyes, let spirits soar,
Where whispers linger evermore.
In this peace, we find our way,
Around the pines, we wish to stay.

Adventures Beneath the Verdant Canopy

Beneath the leaves, where wild things play,
Adventures beckon every day.
In emerald halls, both bold and bright,
We dance with shadows, chasing light.

With every step on forest floor,
A world unfolds, rich with lore.
Creatures peek from behind the trees,
Inviting us to join with ease.

Streams shimmer like a crystal gem,
Reflecting all within their hem.
Every ripple sings a tale,
Of journeys grand beneath the veil.

So gather friends, both old and new,
With laughter bright, as morning dew.
Under the canopy, dreams arise,
Each adventure holds a sweet surprise.

In nature's heart, we find our home,
In every path, we're free to roam.
Adventures call, so let's embrace,
The verdant world, our sacred space.